# Cats and Kittens

By Caryn Jenner

**Senior Editor** Carrie Love
**US Senior Editor** Shannon Beatty
**Project Editor** Kritika Gupta
**Editor** Sophie Parkes
**Assistant Editor** Gunjan Mewati
**Project Art Editor** Polly Appleton
**Art Editor** Mohd Zishan
**Assistant Art Editors** Bhagyashree Nayak, Simran Lakhiani
**Jacket Coordinator** Issy Walsh
**Jacket Designer** Debangshi Basu
**DTP Designers** Dheeraj Singh, Nityanand Kumar
**Picture Researcher** Rituraj Singh
**Senior Production Editor** Jennifer Murray
**Production Controller** Basia Ossowska
**Managing Editors** Penny Smith, Monica Saigal
**Managing Art Editors** Mabel Chan, Ivy Sengupta
**Delhi Team Head** Malavika Talukder
**Publishing Manager** Francesca Young
**Creative Director** Helen Senior
**Publishing Director** Sarah Larter

**Reading Consultant** Dr. Barbara Marinak
**Subject Consultant** Bruce Fogle MBE DVM MRCVS

First American Edition, 2020
Published in the United States by DK Publishing
1450 Broadway, Suite 801, New York, New York 10018

The publisher would like to thank the following for their kind permission to reproduce their photographs:
(Key: a-above; b-below/bottom; c-center; f-far; l-left; r-right; t-top)

**1 Warren Photographic Limited:** Jane Burton (b). **3 Alamy Stock Photo:** Mark Rogers (bl). **Dreamstime.com:** Kristo Robert (cb). **4-5 Dreamstime.com:** Nadezhda Buyanowa. **6 Dreamstime.com:** Azaliya (cb); Ivonne Wierink (c). **7 Alamy Stock Photo:** Juniors Bildarchiv GmbH / F357 (clb). **Dreamstime.com:** Chernetskaya (cb); Viktoria33 (ca). **8-9 Alamy Stock Photo:** EyeEm / Marko Zamurovic. **9 Dreamstime.com:** Slowmotiongli (bl); Ganna Tugolukova (c). **10 Getty Images:** Moment Open / Paolo Carnassale. **11 Dreamstime.com:** Ag042d (cb). **12-13 Dreamstime.com:** Sergey Taran. **13 Dreamstime.com:** Sergey Taran (cr). **14-15 Depositphotos Inc:** EsinDeniz. **16 Dreamstime.com:** Sergiy Bykhunenko (cl). **16-17 Alamy Stock Photo:** Phasin Sudjai. **18 Dreamstime.com:** Oksun70 (b). **19 Dreamstime.com:** Lifeontheside (t). **20 Getty Images:** Stone / GK Hart / Vikki Hart. **23 Dreamstime.com:** Aaron Priestley-wright (ca). **iStockphoto.com:** stock_colors. **24-25 Dreamstime.com:** Pstedrak (b). **25 Dreamstime.com:** Irina Kvyatkovskaya (cr). **26 Alamy Stock Photo:** imageBROKER (b). **27 Alamy Stock Photo:** Bildagentur Geduldig. **28-29 iStockphoto.com:** Nils Jacobi (b). **30 Dreamstime.com:** Photodeti (br); Sonsedskaya (cl). **31 123RF.com:** Eric Isselee (tl). **iStockphoto.com:** totophotos (br). **32 Dreamstime.com:** Galyna Syngaievska (b). **33 Dreamstime.com:** Chernetskaya (b). **34-35 Dreamstime.com:** Chernetskaya (b). **36 Dreamstime.com:** Carlos1967 (cl); Maryna Terletska (cla). **iStockphoto.com:** E+ / MEDITERRANEAN. **37 Dreamstime.com:** Tatyana Mukhomedianova (ca). **38 Dreamstime.com:** Axel Bueckert (bl); Kirill Vorobyev (bc); Isselee (br). **39 Alamy Stock Photo:** Katho Menden (bl). **Dreamstime.com:** Isselee (br). **40 123RF.com:** Duncan Noakes / fouroaks (b). **41 123RF.com:** Anan Kaewkhammul (clb). **Dreamstime.com:** David Burke (cb); Mathias Sunke (t); Ultrashock (bl). **42 123RF.com:** Thorsten Nilson (bl). **Dreamstime.com:** Jeep2499 (br). **43 Dreamstime.com:** Lufimorgan (ca)

**Endpaper images:** *Front:* **Alamy Stock Photo:** Westend61 GmbH / Fotofeeling; *Back:* **Alamy Stock Photo:** Westend61 GmbH / Fotofeeling.

**Cover images:** *Front:* **Warren Photographic Limited:** Mark Taylor (c); *Back:* **Dreamstime.com:** Celso Diniz (ca).

All other images © Dorling Kindersley
For further information see: www.dkimages.com

**For the curious**
**www.dk.com**

# Contents

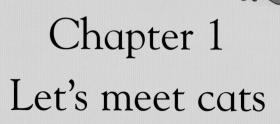

# Chapter 1
# Let's meet cats

Purr, purr. Meow, meow. What's that? It's a cat, of course!

Cats first started living with people around 5,000 years ago.

There are more than 500 million cats around the world. That's a lot! Cats are one of the most popular pets in the world.

Cats are covered in soft fur.
Their fur can be different
colors and patterns. Cats have
sharp claws and sharp teeth.

Tortoiseshell cat

Black and
white cat

They have pointed ears and bright
eyes. Cats have thin, wiry whiskers
that stick out around small noses.
And look at their long tails!

Ginger cat

Colorpointed
cat

Tabby cat

A cat's tail helps it to balance. That's how cats walk in tricky places such as the top of a fence.

Cats walk on their toes. This helps them to balance.

A cat's special muscles mean it can twist around so it usually lands on its feet. Maybe that's why people say that cats have nine lives!

A cat that is angry or scared hisses and arches its back. Its fur stands on end to make it look bigger. Sometimes its ears lie flat against its head too.

A happy cat purrs. It might also push its claws in and out or rub its face against its special human.

Cats rub their heads against people
to show their affection.

# Parts of a cat

Find out more about the special features of a cat.

Cats have powerful hearing. Their ears can point in different directions.

A cat has keen eyes that can see in the dark.

A cat's whiskers act as feelers, helping it detect objects.

A cat's nose has a strong sense of smell.

A cat's long tail shows how it is feeling. This happy cat holds its tail high.

Tiny spikes on a cat's tongue help with grooming and lapping up water.

A cat has thick, padded paws, which help it move silently.

# Chapter 2
# Kittens

A mother cat gives birth to a litter of kittens. There can be as many as ten kittens in a litter! Usually, there are only four to six kittens. The kittens stay near their mother to keep warm. They feed on her milk.

Newborn kittens often purr while feeding.

A newborn kitten is so small that it can lie in your hand. Newborn kittens can't see or hear.

A newborn kitten

Their eyes and ears will open at about two weeks old. At about three weeks old, kittens start walking.

Newborn kittens snuggle together to stay warm.

Soon kittens learn to run and jump and play. They also get used to being around humans.

Always be gentle with cats and kittens.

A mother with her kitten

Kittens should stay with their mother until they are about ten weeks old. Then they can leave their mother to be someone's pet.

Oops! This kitten knocks over a vase of flowers.

Kittens have lots and lots of energy! They run around quickly, but they can be clumsy and knock things over. Kittens are very curious, too. They like exploring new things. This can get them into trouble!

These kittens jump in and out of the basket.

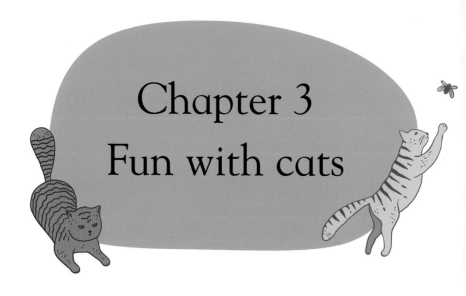

# Chapter 3
# Fun with cats

Cats love to play. It's good exercise. They like to run and climb. They like to hide and roll around.

Sometimes cats pretend they are hunting. They chase toys and pounce on them! Sometimes they hunt for real and catch birds and mice.

This cat chases a red ball.

23

Cats spend most of their day sleeping. They might sleep curled up in a ball or stretched out in the sun. Cats often take quick catnaps.

Cats spend two-thirds of their lives sleeping!

Sometimes, their tails and ears twitch when they sleep. Do you think these cats are dreaming?

Cats stay clean by grooming themselves. They lick their fur and paws, which keeps them cool. Sometimes cats groom each other.

Cats keep their claws trimmed by scratching. When they're outdoors, they scratch on trees and fences. They should have a scratching post to use indoors.

Cats like to have their own
territory. Some cats explore a
wide area. Other cats stay closer
to home.

This cat has entered the
other cat's territory.
The other cat chases
it away.

A cat might hiss and chase strange cats away from its territory. Sometimes, cats fight over their territory.

# Crazy about cats

Find out some fun facts about cats.

While cats usually live to be 15–20 years old, a cat called Creme Puff lived to be 38 years old!

Cats and dogs often become best friends.

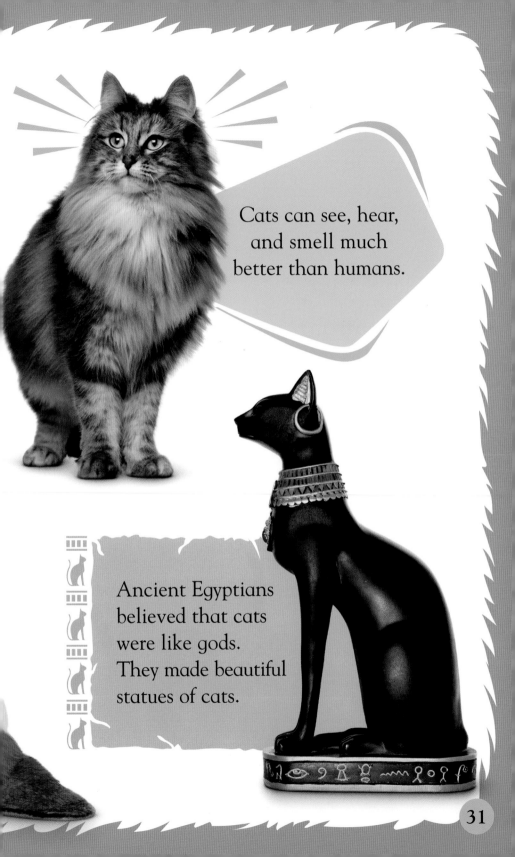

Cats can see, hear, and smell much better than humans.

Ancient Egyptians believed that cats were like gods. They made beautiful statues of cats.

# Chapter 4
# Caring for
# a pet cat

Feed your cat at least twice a
day. Most cats eat wet food, made
from chunks of meat or fish. They
also eat dry, savory biscuits.
They drink fresh water.

Cats need a litter box to use as a toilet. Fill the box with about 4 in (10 cm) of litter. Scoop out dirty litter after a cat uses it.

Most cats get used to their litter box very easily.

Take your cat to the vet every year for a checkup and vaccinations. Your cat also needs regular treatment to protect it from fleas and worms.

Ask your vet whenever you have a question about your cat.

Cats show how they are feeling with their body language.

Like humans, cats have moods. Sometimes, your cat might jump on your lap or want to play. Other times, it might want to be left alone.

Always be gentle with cats. An unhappy cat can scratch you with its claws.

# Cat breeds

Different breeds are different sizes.
Many cats are a mix of breeds.

Siamese

Abyssinian

Persian

Maine coon

European domestic shorthair

39

# Chapter 5
# Big cats

Cats belong to a family of mammals known as felines. There are 37 types of felines. They all have sharp claws and sharp teeth.

Lion

Leopard

Most felines have long tails. They are good at running, climbing, and hunting.

Lions and leopards are felines. Here are some others.

Jaguar

Bobcat

Mountain lion

Pet cats are the smallest type of feline. Tigers are the biggest. These two felines have a lot in common.

Which type of feline would you rather have as a pet?

Tiger

Ginger cat

Would you want a big, fierce tiger as a pet? Of course not. A small cat makes a great pet!

# Quiz

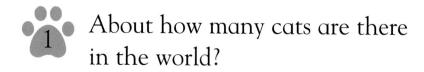

**1** About how many cats are there in the world?

**2** Why might a cat hiss and arch its back?

**3** What do a cat's whiskers do?

**4** About how old are kittens when their eyes and ears open?

**5** How much of their lives do cats spend sleeping?

**6** How do cats stay clean?

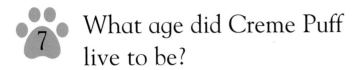

**7** What age did Creme Puff live to be?

**8** How often should you feed your cat?

**9** Which family of mammals do cats belong to?

# Glossary

**breed**
A type of cat with special features.

**feline**
A part of the cat family, such as a tiger.

**groom**
To keep a cat clean.

**pounce**
To jump on something.

**savory**
A taste that is not sweet.

**territory**
An area that a cat thinks of as its own.

**vaccination**
A way of preventing certain illnesses.

**vet**
A doctor for animals.

**wiry**
Like wire, a cat's whiskers are thin
and stiff.

# Index

# A LEVEL FOR EVERY READER

This book is a part of an exciting four-level reading series to support children in developing the habit of reading widely for both pleasure and information. Each book is designed to develop a child's reading skills, fluency, grammar awareness, and comprehension in order to build confidence and enjoyment when reading.

### Ready for a Level 2 (Beginning to Read) book

A child should:

- be able to recognize a bank of common words quickly and be able to blend sounds together to make some words.
- be familiar with using beginner letter sounds and context clues to figure out unfamiliar words.
- sometimes correct their reading if it doesn't look right or make sense.
- be aware of the need for a slight pause at commas and a longer one at periods.

### A valuable and shared reading experience

For many children, reading requires much effort, but adult participation can make reading both fun and easier. Here are a few tips on how to use this book with a young reader:

*Check out the contents together:*
- read about the book on the back cover and talk about the contents page to help heighten interest and expectation.
- discuss new or difficult words.
- talk about labels, annotations, and pictures.

*Support the reader:*
- tell the child the title and help them predict what the book will be about.
- give the book to the young reader to turn the pages.
- where necessary, encourage longer words to be broken into syllables, sound out each one, and then flow the syllables together; ask the child to reread the sentence to check the meaning.
- encourage the reader to vary their voice as they read; demonstrate how to do this, if helpful.

*Talk at the end of each page:*
- ask questions about the text and the meaning of some of the words used—this helps develop comprehension skills.
- read the quiz at the end of the book and encourage the reader to answer the questions, if necessary, by turning back to the relevant pages to find the answers.

Reading consultant: Dr. Barbara Marinak, Dean and Professor of Education at Mount St. Mary's University, Maryland.